Zest–scrape the
topmost layer of skin
of a lemon or orange to use
for extra flavour

A shallow metal dish
with about 2½ cm (1 in) of hot water
in it will serve as a bain-marie for slow moist cooking

Contents

Note:
For the purposes of this book, 25 grams (g) = 1 ounce (oz),
500 millilitres (ml) = 1 pint (pt), 5 millilitres = one level teaspoon (tsp)
and 15 millilitres = one level tablespoon (tbs).

First edition

© LADYBIRD BOOKS LTD MCMLXXXIV

All rights reserved. No part of this publication may be reproduced, stored in a retrieval system, or transmitted in any form or by any means, electronic, mechanical, photo-copying, recording or otherwise, without the prior consent of the copyright owner.

Hot Puddings and Cold Sweets

by KATE HUTCHINSON
photographs by TIM CLARK

Ladybird Books Loughborough

Caramel Oranges (serves 4)

4 oranges
150 g (6 oz) granulated sugar
30 ml (2 tablespoonfuls) cold water

1 Peel all skin and pith from the oranges.
2 Slice oranges, removing any pips, and arrange in a flat serving dish.
3 Make the caramel (see opposite) and pour it immediately over the sliced oranges. (It will set straightaway, but then gradually dissolve.)
4 Leave for 1-2 hours before serving with lightly whipped cream.

To make caramel

1 Put sugar and water in a thick bottomed pan and stir over heat until sugar is dissolved.

2 Steadily boil without stirring until the syrup thickens and the bubbling slows.

3 Once the syrup begins to turn colour (about 5 minutes) it will brown *very* quickly.

4 As soon as it is the colour of a ginger biscuit it is ready and must be used straightaway.

Note Care must be taken not to allow the caramel to burn. Even with the heat turned off it will continue cooking with the heat of the pan.

Do not attempt to scrape the last bit of caramel out of the pan. Just fill the pan with very hot water and leave to soak – the caramel will dissolve without difficulty.

Iced Coffee Charlotte (serves 6)

10 sponge fingers, each cut in half
30 ml (2 tablespoonfuls) warmed apricot jam
2 eggs, separated
15 ml (1 tablespoonful) coffee powder
15 ml (1 tablespoonful) sweet sherry
60 ml (4 tablespoonfuls) icing sugar
125 ml (¼ pt) double cream lightly whipped

1 Line a 15 cm (6 in) loose-bottomed cake tin with non-stick paper.
2 Dip the half fingers in the jam and arrange them around the sides of the tin, rounded ends down.
3 Whisk egg whites until stiff, then whisk in half the icing sugar, and whisk again until *very* stiff.
4 Whisk the egg yolks together with the rest of the icing sugar and the coffee powder dissolved in the sherry.
5 Combine the two mixtures, stirring gently.
6 Fold in the cream.
7 Pour into the prepared tin and level off.
8 Freeze until firm.
9 Turn out and decorate with rosettes of cream and chocolate rose leaves or triangles (optional).
10 Serve straightaway, or put back into freezer until needed.

Chocolate Leaves

Chocolate leaves make a delightful decoration.
Make a supply during the summer.

1 Collect some undamaged rose leaves of similar sizes, and wash and dry them.
2 Melt some plain chocolate on a plate over hot water.
3 Drag the separate leaves over the chocolate turning the coated side uppermost and leave on a cooling tray to set.
4 Gently peel off the leaf and store the chocolate leaves in a plastic box in the fridge. I layer mine between kitchen paper. They will keep until the following year if not used up.

Snow Queen (serves 6)

250 ml (½ pt) double cream

15 ml (1 tablespoonful) icing sugar

100 g (4 oz) broken meringues

30 ml (2 tablespoonfuls) orange juice or sieved raspberry purée (see note)

1 Whisk the cream stiffly, add the sugar and chosen flavouring.
2 Fold in the meringues.
3 Pour into a lightly oiled plastic basin or mould.
4 Cover with clingfilm and freeze.
5 Turn on to a plate and thaw for 15 minutes.
6 Decorate with sweetened raspberries or Kiwi fruit.

Note To make purée, cook 50 g (2 oz) raspberries in a tiny drop of water until soft, then press through a sieve.

Satsuma Ices (serves 8-10)

8-10 satsumas
150 g (6 oz) caster
sugar
250 ml (½ pt) water

Juice and zest of
1 lemon
2 egg whites
1 small carton double
cream

1 Put sugar and water in a pan and warm gently until the sugar has dissolved, then increase heat and boil steadily for 10 minutes. Leave to cool.

2 Wash the satsumas and slice off the tops, saving them for later use. Scoop out the flesh with a teaspoon, taking care not to damage the skins.

3 Liquidise the satsuma flesh together with the lemon juice.

4 Strain into the cold syrup and add the lemon zest (see front endpaper).

5 Pour into a plastic bowl or box and freeze until slushy.

6 Whisk the egg whites stiffly and fold into the fruit ice.

7 Return to freezer until almost frozen.

8 Stir the fruit ice briskly, and then stir in the stiffly whipped cream.

9 Spoon the ice cream into the fruit skins until very full. Replace the 'lids'.

10 Open freeze until very firm.

11 Wrap separately in clingfilm and pack in a box.

12 Remove from freezer 20 minutes before required. Serve on a plate decorated with fresh leaves.

Peach and Yogurt Brulée (serves 4)

2 ripe peaches
2.5 ml (½ teaspoonful)
ground ginger
1 small carton plain set
yogurt

1 small carton whipping
cream
50-75 g (2-3 oz)
demerara sugar
4 meringue shells

1 Peel, stone and slice peaches into a fireproof dish (or small dishes).
2 Sprinkle with ground ginger.
3 Whip cream stiffly and fold in the yogurt and broken meringue shells.
4 Smooth over the top of the peaches.
5 Sprinkle thickly with brown sugar, completely covering the cream.
6 Put under a very hot grill until sugar melts.
7 Chill for 1-2 hours.

Iced Cherry and Pineapple Crunch (serves 8)

100 g (4 oz) digestive biscuits (crushed)

100 g (4 oz) plain cooking chocolate

15 ml (1 tablespoonful) golden syrup

8 pineapple rings (6 of them chopped finely)

25 g (1 oz) butter

16 maraschino cherries (10 of them chopped)

15 ml (1 tablespoonful) lemon juice

15 ml (1 tablespoonful) icing sugar

125 ml (¼ pt) double cream

1 Gently melt the chocolate, syrup and butter in a pan and stir in the crushed biscuits.
2 Press into a lined and oiled swiss roll tin.
3 Whip the cream and fold in the chopped fruit, icing sugar and lemon juice.
4 Spread over the biscuit base and level out.
5 Freeze until needed.
6 Allow to soften for 15 minutes, then cut into wedges. Decorate with the two remaining pineapple slices and the remaining cherries.
7 Serve while still partly frozen.

Prune and Orange Yogurt Whip

(serves 4)

1 tall tin of prunes
2 cartons of orange yogurt
1 egg white
1 carton (5 fl oz) whipping cream, whipped
Few flaked almonds (browned under the grill)

1 Drain prune juice into liquidiser, and then remove stones from the prunes.
2 Add the stoned prunes and the yogurt to the liquidiser and purée.
3 Whisk the egg white until stiff.
4 Add the prune and yogurt mixture to the egg white and fold gently together.
5 Divide the prune whip between 4 pretty glasses layering it with the cream.
6 Scatter the toasted almond flakes on top.
7 Chill and serve within 2-3 hours.

Lemon Cream (serves 4)

1 egg white whisked stiffly
1 small carton of double cream whipped stiffly
45 ml (3 tablespoonfuls) lemon curd

1 Stir all ingredients together gently.
2 Pile into long-stemmed glasses, and decorate with lemon.
3 Chill and serve.

Damson Fool (serves 6)

Fruit Purée

450 g (1 lb approx) ripe damsons

30 ml (2 tablespoonfuls) water

75-100 g (3-4 oz) sugar

Custard

30 ml (2 tablespoonfuls) custard powder

30 ml (2 tablespoonfuls) sugar

250 ml (½ pt) milk

Topping

1 small carton of whipping cream – whipped

1 Wash and destalk the fruit.
2 Simmer the water and damsons in a pan until very soft. Stir occasionally.

3 Press the softened fruit through a sieve to make a purée, and remove stones.
4 Stir the sugar into the purée and check for sweetness.
5 Make a thick custard by putting the custard powder, sugar and milk into a pan and stir to remove any lumps. Then boil until thickened, stirring all the time.
6 Mix the damson purée into the custard.
7 Pour into one large glass dish or into six smaller ones.
8 Leave for 3-4 hours to cool and set.
9 Pipe a whorl of cream on top. Add chocolate rose leaves or other decoration as preferred, and serve.

Try substituting gooseberries, rhubarb or apricots when damsons are not available. A few drops of green food colouring improves Gooseberry Fool.

Gâteau McMahon (serves 10)

Fresh or frozen strawberries liquidised to make 250 ml
(½ pt) and 10 whole strawberries

1 sachet (3 teaspoonfuls) gelatine

75 ml (3 tablespoonfuls) hot water

100 g (4 oz) sugar

2 egg whites

250 ml (½ pt) double cream whipped, and 125 ml (¼ pt)
double cream to decorate

2 thin circles of shortbread (one whole and one cut into
10 fan shapes)

1 Put one circle of shortbread into base of a lined loose-bottomed 24 cm (9½ in) cake tin (use Bakewell paper).

2 Dissolve gelatine in the hot water as directed on the packet.

3 Stir in the sugar until dissolved, then stir in the liquidised strawberries.

4 When cool and just beginning to set, fold in the whipped cream and then the lightly whisked egg whites.

5 Pour into the prepared tin on top of the shortbread, and leave to set.

6 Turn out on to a plate, and arrange the fans of shortbread at angles, supported by rosettes of whipped cream and whole strawberries.

Note Raspberries are equally suitable for this recipe.

Caramel Egg Custards (serves 6)

Custard
4 (size 3) eggs
500 ml (1 pt) milk,
slightly warmed
100 g (4 oz) sugar

Caramel
150 g (6 oz) granulated sugar
30 ml (2 tablespoonfuls) cold water

1 Grease a ¾ litre (1½ pt) basin or 6 dariole moulds with a little butter.
2 Make caramel as described on page 5, and pour into bottom of chosen dish or moulds.
3 Beat the eggs and sugar together, and mix thoroughly with the warmed milk.
4 Strain through a sieve into the basin or moulds.
5 Stand in a shallow tin (a bain-marie–see front endpaper) containing 2½ cm (1 in) of water.
6 Bake gently in centre of oven at gas mark 4 (electricity 350°F/180°C) for approximately 45-60 minutes until set (individual custards will take less time*).
7 Allow to cool.
8 Leave in fridge or some other cold place until the following day.
9 Turn out onto a serving dish. (The caramel will have made a rich liquid sauce.)

Note *To test if egg custard is baked, plunge the tip of a knife into the centre of the custard. If it comes out clean, the custard is set.

Barbara's Chocolate Layer Pudding (serves 4)

Pudding

100 g (4 oz) self raising flour
15 ml (1 tablespoonful) cocoa
50 g (2 oz) sugar
25 g (1 oz) margarine
25 g (1 oz) coconut
125 ml (¼ pt) milk

Topping

50 g (2 oz) demerara sugar
15 ml (1 tablespoonful) cocoa
10 ml (2 teaspoonfuls) coffee powder
250 ml (½ pt) boiling water

1 Light oven gas mark 4 (electricity 350°F/180°C).

2 Grease a ½ litre (1 pt) soufflé dish.

3 Sieve the flour and rub in the margarine.

4 Add the sugar, coconut and sieved cocoa.

5 Add the milk to make a soft mix.

6 Spread in dish.

7 Cover this mixture with topping mixture of demerara sugar, cocoa and coffee.

8 Pour the boiling water over the topping.

9 Stand dish in a shallow baking tin (a bain-marie –see front endpaper) containing 2½ cm (1 in) of water.

10 Bake for 45 minutes in the centre of the oven.

Note The pudding will have a liquid sauce underneath.

Bishop's Pudding (serves 4)

500 ml (1 pt) milk   *50 g (2 oz) walnut halves*
50 g (2 oz) semolina   *50 g (2 oz) marmalade*
50 g (2 oz) sugar   *1 egg*

1 Boil milk and sugar together.
2 Sprinkle semolina over the surface of milk and stir.
3 Cook gently, stirring all the time, for 5 minutes or until thickened.
4 Remove from heat and allow to cool for a few minutes.
5 Add the beaten egg, marmalade and roughly chopped nuts.
6 Pour into a greased pie dish.
7 Bake gas mark 4 (electricity 350°F/180°C) for 20 minutes in the centre of the oven.

Special Bread and Butter Pudding (serves 4)

4 thin slices of well
buttered bread
(brown or white)
cut into triangles
250 ml (½ pt) milk
2 eggs (size 3)

50 g (2 oz) sugar
50 g (2 oz) dried
fruit (optional)
Zest of 1 orange
(see front endpaper)
A little demerara sugar

1 Grease an ovenproof dish and light oven gas mark 5 (electricity 375°F/190°C).

2 Layer triangles of bread and butter with dried fruit and orange zest, finishing with a decorative top layer of triangles.

3 Warm milk gently, and stir in the sugar until dissolved.

4 Add to the beaten eggs.

5 Strain custard over the layered triangles.

6 Sprinkle with demerara sugar.

7 Bake in the centre of the oven until browned and set, approximately 30-40 minutes.

Father's Delight (serves 4-6)

100 g (4 oz) self raising flour
5 ml (1 teaspoonful) baking powder
100 g (4 oz) caster sugar
100 g (4 oz) soft margarine

2 eggs (size 3)
1 large Bramley apple, peeled, cored and sliced
2.5 ml (½ teaspoonful) ground cinnamon mixed with 2.5 ml (½ teaspoonful) sugar

1 Grease an ovenproof dish and light oven on gas mark 4 (electricity 350°F/180°C).
2 Sieve flour and baking powder into mixing bowl.
3 Add the sugar, margarine and eggs.
4 Beat well until thoroughly mixed.
5 Spoon into greased dish, and level.
6 Spike the sponge mixture with slices of apple.
7 Sprinkle the apple with cinnamon topping.
8 Bake in centre of oven until well risen and spongy, approximately 40-45 minutes.
9 Serve hot with custard.

Fruit Fritters

(serves 4)

Fritter batter
100 g (4 oz) plain flour
2 egg whites and 1 egg yolk
125 ml (¼ pt) cold water

Marinade
30 ml (2 tablespoonfuls) water
*15 ml (1 tablespoonful)
lemon juice*
15 ml (1 tablespoonful) sugar

Suggested fruit
Apple slices
Victoria plum halves
Pineapple slices
Banana pieces

1 Leave prepared fruit in marinade for a short time while the batter is prepared.
2 Make the batter, *without* the egg whites, by stirring the water and egg yolk into the flour to make a smooth thick mixture.
3 Stir in the marinade and add the softly whisked egg whites.
4 Dip the marinaded fruit into the batter and fry a few at a time for 3-4 minutes in deep fat, without the frying basket.
5 Drain on crumpled kitchen roll and serve immediately with sugar and cream.

St Clement's Sponge Pudding

(serves 4-6)

100 g (4 oz) self raising flour

5 ml (1 teaspoonful) baking powder

100 g (4 oz) caster sugar

100 g (4 oz) margarine

2 eggs (size 3)

1 thin-skinned orange

1 thin-skinned lemon

25-50 g (1-2 oz) demerara sugar

1 Light oven on gas mark 4 (electricity 350°F/180°C).

28

2 Grease a ring mould thoroughly, and sprinkle thickly with demerara sugar.

3 Arrange some thin orange and lemon slices in a decorative pattern in the tin.

4 Sieve the flour and baking powder into a mixing bowl. Add the sugar, margarine and eggs, and beat until well mixed.

5 Spoon into the ring mould.

6 Bake in centre of oven for 25-30 minutes, until well risen and spongy to the touch.

7 Turn out on to a warm serving dish.

8 Serve with pouring cream or the following sauce.

Marmalade Sauce

15 ml (1 tablespoonful) cornflour

2 heaped tablespoonfuls marmalade

1 Add any juice from left-over orange and lemon to the marmalade, and make it up to 250 ml (½ pt) with cold water.

2 Add the cornflour and stir until there are no lumps.

3 Boil until thickened.

Baked Chocolate Alaska (serves 6)

1 sponge flan case
1 tin pear halves
1 block of chocolate ice cream
3 egg whites
150 g (6 oz) caster sugar
To decorate
angelica, glacé cherries

1 Light oven gas mark 7 (electricity 425°F/220°C).

2 Place flan case on an ovenproof plate.

3 Arrange drained pear halves in centre of flan.

4 Make meringue:
   a) Whisk egg whites until they are very stiff and will stand in points.
   b) Add half the measured sugar and whisk again until very firm and stiff.
   c) With the utmost care, gently fold in the remainder of the sugar. DO NOT STIR MORE THAN NECESSARY.

5 Take ice cream from freezer and pack on top of the pear halves.

6 Cover the flan and ice cream completely with the meringue making sure that no ice cream is left uncovered.

7 Swirl the meringue, and decorate with spikes of angelica and pieces of cherry.

8 Place in centre of hot oven for 3-4 minutes until meringue is attractively browned.

9 Serve immediately, otherwise the ice cream melts.

Treacle Tart (serves 4)

Pastry

150 g (6 oz) plain flour

Large pinch of salt

50 g (2 oz) block of margarine

25 g (1 oz) lard

30 ml (2 tablespoonfuls) iced water

Filling

50 g (2 oz) freshly crumbed bread

45 ml (3 tablespoonfuls) golden syrup

15 ml (1 tablespoonful) black treacle

30 ml (2 tablespoonfuls) marmalade

1 Light oven gas mark 6 (electricity 400°F/200°C).

2 Rub fats into flour and salt until it resembles breadcrumbs.

3 Add all the water, and mix to a stiff paste.

4 Roll into a good circle and cover a 22 cm (9 in) ovenproof plate with it.

5 Trim off the surplus and decorate by fluting the edge or by cutting and folding over.

6 Melt the syrup, treacle and marmalade gently in a pan and stir in the breadcrumbs.

7 Spread filling over pastry centre.

8 Roll trimmings very thinly, and cut strips to

make a wheel pattern on top of the filling.
9 Bake on centre shelf for approximately 20-25
minutes until pastry edges are browned.
10 Serve hot with custard or eat sliced cold.

Bramley and Walnut Cream Flan

(serves 6-8)

Shortcrust pastry made from 200 g (8 oz) plain flour

450 g (1 lb) Bramley cooking apples

50 g (2 oz) butter

50 g (2 oz) sugar

Zest and juice of 1 lemon

2 pinches grated nutmeg

3 digestive biscuits (crushed)

2 egg yolks

50 g (2 oz) walnuts

1 small carton of whipping cream

1 Light the oven on gas mark 6 (electricity 400°F/200°C).

2 Roll out pastry and line a 22 cm (9 in) flan dish or ring and bake blind for 10 minutes till half baked.

3 Peel and core apples, then cook with lemon juice until very soft.

4 Sieve.

5 Add butter and sugar to the hot purée.

6 Stir in the zest (see front endpaper), nutmeg and biscuit crumbs.

7 Lightly whip the cream and stir in the egg yolks.

8 Stir into apple mixture and pour into pastry case.

9 Make a lattice pattern with very thin strips of pastry and arrange walnuts in the spaces.

10 Bake in centre of oven for 20-25 minutes.

Note This flan is equally nice hot or cold.

Steamed Raspberry Sponge

(serves 4-6)

2 eggs (size 3)
100 g (4 oz) self raising flour
5 ml (1 teaspoonful) baking powder

100 g (4 oz) caster sugar
100 g (4 oz) soft tub margarine
*45 ml (3 tablespoonfuls) raspberry jam ** *

1 Set a large pan of water to boil.
2 Grease a ¾ litre (1½ pt) basin, and put jam in the bottom.
3 Sieve flour and baking powder into a mixing bowl.
4 Add sugar, margarine and eggs.
5 Beat everything together until thoroughly mixed (about 2 minutes).
6 Spoon sponge mixture on top of jam. (The basin should be ½-⅔rds full.)
7 Cover with greased paper or foil, pleated to allow the pudding to rise, and press closely to the basin or tie with string.

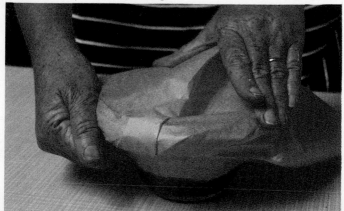

8 Put in steamer and cover with lid.

9 Put steamer over gently boiling water (see note below).

10 Steam for 1¼ hours or pressure cook for 35 minutes.

11 Remove foil and turn the pudding out on to a warmed plate.

12 Serve hot with custard.

Note Do not allow pan to boil dry. Top up with boiling water if necessary.

*Substitute lemon curd, marmalade or golden syrup for jam.

Pancakes (makes 8 pancakes)

Batter

100 g (4 oz) plain flour   250 ml (½ pt) milk
Pinch of salt   25 g (1 oz) lard
1 egg (size 3)

1 Sieve flour and salt into a bowl and make a well
   in the centre.
2 Drop in the egg and half the milk. Using either a
   wooden spoon, or a hand-held electric whisk,
   gradually mix together. (Or put all ingredients in
   a liquidiser and mix.)

3 Beat until smooth and then stir in the rest of the milk. If covered, this batter will keep for up to 24 hours in the fridge.

4 Divide the lard into eight pieces.

5 Melt one piece of lard in a nonstick frying pan and allow to get really hot.

6 Pour in enough batter to coat the bottom of the pan thinly, tilting it to allow the batter to flow evenly.

7 Fry until golden brown underneath and the batter is just set (approximately 2 minutes). Shake pan gently so that the pancake becomes loose.

8 Flip over with a fish slice and fry the other side.

9 Repeat to make 7 more pancakes.

10 Layer up the cooked pancakes with greaseproof paper until all the batter is used up.

Shrove Tuesday Pancakes

Serve sprinkled with sugar and freshly squeezed lemon or orange juice.

Stuffed Pancakes

1 Put a spoonful of cherry pie filling or some hot apple purée with raisins on each pancake, and roll up and arrange in a greased ovenproof dish.

2 Sprinkle with sugar and grill for 3-5 minutes to reheat.

3 Serve with lightly whipped cream.

Lemon Dainty Pudding (serves 4)

500 ml (1 pt) milk
50 g (2 oz) margarine
50 g (2 oz) plain flour

50 g (2 oz) sugar
Zest and juice of 2 lemons
3 eggs separated

1 Light oven on gas mark 4 (electricity 350°F/180°C).
2 Mix together the flour, margarine, sugar, egg yolks, zest (see front endpaper) and lemon juice.
3 Stir in the milk thoroughly.
4 Whisk the egg whites, and fold into the mixture.
5 Pour into a greased soufflé dish.
6 Stand in a shallow tin (bain-marie – see front endpaper) containing 2½ cm (1 in) of water.
7 Bake for approximately 45-55 minutes on the middle shelf.

Note The pudding separates into 2 layers; light sponge on top and a creamy lemon sauce beneath.

Christmas Pudding with Egg Nog Sauce (serves 6-8)

100 g (4 oz) fresh white or wholemeal breadcrumbs

100 g (4 oz) suet

100 g (4 oz) brown sugar

25 g (1 oz) plain flour

450 g (1 lb) mixed dried fruit

25 g (1 oz) glacé cherries (optional)

25 g (1 oz) nuts (optional)

5 ml (1 teaspoonful) mixed spice

1 lemon

1 medium carrot

1 medium apple

2 eggs (size 3)

30 ml (2 tablespoonfuls) milk or alcohol

1 Cut two circles of greaseproof paper, to fit the top and bottom of a 750 ml (1½ pt) basin.

2 Grease basin and put small circle of paper in the bottom and regrease.
3 Grate lemon zest into large mixing bowl and add the juice.

4 Peel and grate the apple and carrot into same bowl.

5 Add all other ingredients *except* the egg and liquid.

6 Mix thoroughly.

7 Add beaten eggs and liquid.

8 Mix again and remember to wish!

9 Press well into basin, and level.

10 Cover with other greased paper circle and a piece of foil.

11 Steam for 6 hours, or pressure cook for 3 hours.

12 Cover with fresh dry foil, and keep in a cool dry place until needed.

13 Reheat when needed by steaming for 1 hour, by pressure cooking for half an hour, or by microwaving for 4 minutes.

14 Serve with Egg Nog Sauce.

Egg Nog Sauce

2 eggs separated
100 g (4 oz) caster sugar
1 large carton of whipping cream

2.5 ml (½ teaspoonful) vanilla

2.5 ml (½ teaspoonful) rum essence

1 Whisk the cream until stiff.

2 Beat the egg yolks with 50 g (2 oz) sugar.

3 Whisk the egg whites stiffly and fold in 50 g (2 oz) sugar.

4 Combine all three mixtures together with either the vanilla or the rum essence.

5 Chill and serve.

Index